EXPERIMENT WITH MOVEMENT

Written by **Bryan Murphy**

Science Consultant Dr Christine Sutton
Nuclear Physics Department, University of Oxford
Education Consultant Ruth Bessant

TWO-CAN/WATTS

First published in Great Britain in 1991 by
Two-Can Publishing Ltd
346 Old Street, London EC1V 9NQ

This edition published in 1995 by
Two-Can Publishing Ltd in association with
Watts Books

Copyright © Two-Can Publishing Ltd, 1991
Text copyright © Bryan Murphy, 1991
Design by Linda Blakemore
Printed in Hong Kong

4 6 8 10 9 7 5 3

All rights reserved. No part of this publication may be reproduced, stored
in a retrieval system, or transmitted in any form or by any means,
electronic, mechanical, photocopying or otherwise, without prior
written permission of the copyright owner.

The JUMP! logo and the word JUMP! are registered trade marks.

British Library Cataloguing in Publication Data

Murphy, Bryan
 Experiment with Movement
 1. Motion. Experiments
 I. Title
531'.11'0724

ISBN 1-85434-063-8

All photographs are copyright © Fiona Pragoff, except for the following: Cover ZEFA Picture Library (UK) Ltd p.4 (left) ZEFA Picture Library (UK) Ltd (top right) Frank Lane Picture Agency (bottom right) Frank Lane Picture Agency p.5 (top left) Ford Motor Co. (UK) (bottom) ZEFA Picture Library (UK) Ltd p.16 All Sport Photographic Ltd p.17 (top) ZEFA Picture Library (UK) Ltd p.18 Science Photo Library/David Parker p.19 (top left) ZEFA Picture Library (UK) Ltd (bottom) Science Photo Library/ Dr Jeremy Burgess p.20 Science Photo Library/Charles Falco p.21 (left) ZEFA Picture Library (UK) Ltd p.22 Science Photo Library/John Sanford p.26 Rex Features London p.28 ZEFA Picture Library (UK) Ltd.

The photograph on page 21 is used with the permission of LEGO UK Ltd. LEGO ® is a registered trade mark, the property of the LEGO group

All illustrations by Sally Kindberg. Edited by Monica Byles.

Thanks to the staff and pupils of St Thomas' C.E. Primary School, London W10

CONTENTS

What is movement?	4
Where do forces come from?	6
Forces at work	8
How do we move?	10
Forces in the playground	12
Slowing down	14
Moving fast	16
Big machines	18
Gearwheels are great	20
Rollers and pulleys	22
Levers	24
Fast food	26
Gravity	28
Glossary	30
Index	32

All words marked in **bold** can be found in the glossary

WHAT IS MOVEMENT?

Sit very still and look around you. What do you notice? Is anything **moving**? You may have to look very carefully but most things move.

Some things move very quickly, like **rockets** and aeroplanes. Flying birds and cars move much more slowly but are quite fast when compared to real slowcoaches like snails.

Here are some pictures of things that move. Put them in order, with the fastest ones first.

WHERE DO FORCES COME FROM?

Everything that moves does so because of something called a **force**. Without forces, the world would be a very boring place. Imagine what it would be like if everything stayed exactly where it was. Forces can also hurt you, so be very careful when you do any of the experiments in this book.

Here is a way of making an indoor rocket. You will need a long piece of thin string, a straw cut in half (not lengthwise), and a sausage-shaped balloon.

● Thread the string through the half straw and tie it tightly between two chairs.
● Blow up the balloon and keep the neck pinched between your fingers.
● Ask a helper carefully to tape the bottom side of the balloon (along the long edge) to the straw, while you continue to pinch the neck of the balloon to keep the air in.
● Quickly let go of the balloon.

What happened? As the air in the balloon escaped, it pushed the rocket forwards along the string. Try using a different-shaped balloon or different types and thicknesses of string.

This is an experiment to make a wind-up toy. You will need an old cotton reel, an **elastic** band, half of a used match, a candle and a whole used match.

● Ask an adult to cut a slice from the end of the candle.
● Smooth off the round faces as much as possible on newspaper or sugar paper.
● Ask an adult to bore a hole through the middle of the candle slice.

● Loop the elastic band through the cotton reel and candle slice. Hold the band in position at the opposite end from the candle slice with the half matchstick.
● Fix the elastic band next to the candle slice with the match.
● Make sure that the match is rubbing against the smooth wax.
● Wind the elastic band tight against the candle slice using the match to turn it.
● Put the toy on a table, let go and watch what happens. The **energy** stored in the wound-up elastic pushes the car forwards.

FORCES AT WORK

If a force pushes or pulls something, there are different things that could happen. You can create forces to move and shape things yourself. When you make something out of modelling clay, you are using different forces. You can push the clay between your fingers to flatten it; and you can squeeze and pull the clay apart to make it into long sausages. How many different shapes can you make?

You can make your own **windmill** from thin card, two beads, a long pin and some wood.

▶ Trace this shape on to card and paint the card in different colours on both sides. Cut along the lines, then bend each vane into the centre without making a sharp, folded edge. Ask an adult to pin the windmill on to the wooden handle between the two beads so that it can spin freely.

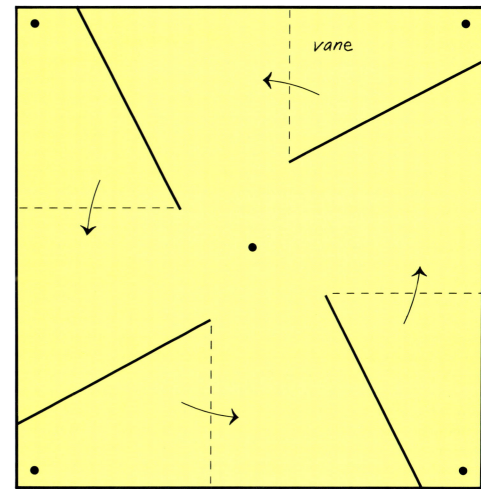

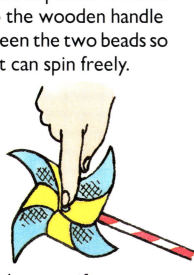

What happens if you move your windmill through the air? The air pushes it round, and makes a force which lets it spin. See if you can make the windmill move even better by making the vanes bigger or by changing their shape.

9

HOW DO WE MOVE?

It is very difficult to sit still for a long time. We are always moving. We can walk, run, jump, climb and swim. How many other ways of moving can you think of?

How do we move? This girl has a strong **skeleton**, which gives her the right shape. Her bones are joined in many ways so that she can move. She has **joints** that bend, like elbows and knees, and some that rotate, like wrists and ankles. Her shoulder is also a joint that can twist. **Muscles** are attached to her bones to make them move.

To make your body work properly, you need a supply of good food. There are more than 600 muscles in your body pulling on your bones to make them work.

Try making a model arm to see how the muscles work. You will need some thick card, a split pin and two elastic bands.

Cut these shapes out of thick card using the templates and make an elbow joint out of a split pin. The joint will bend, but we need some muscles to provide the forces.

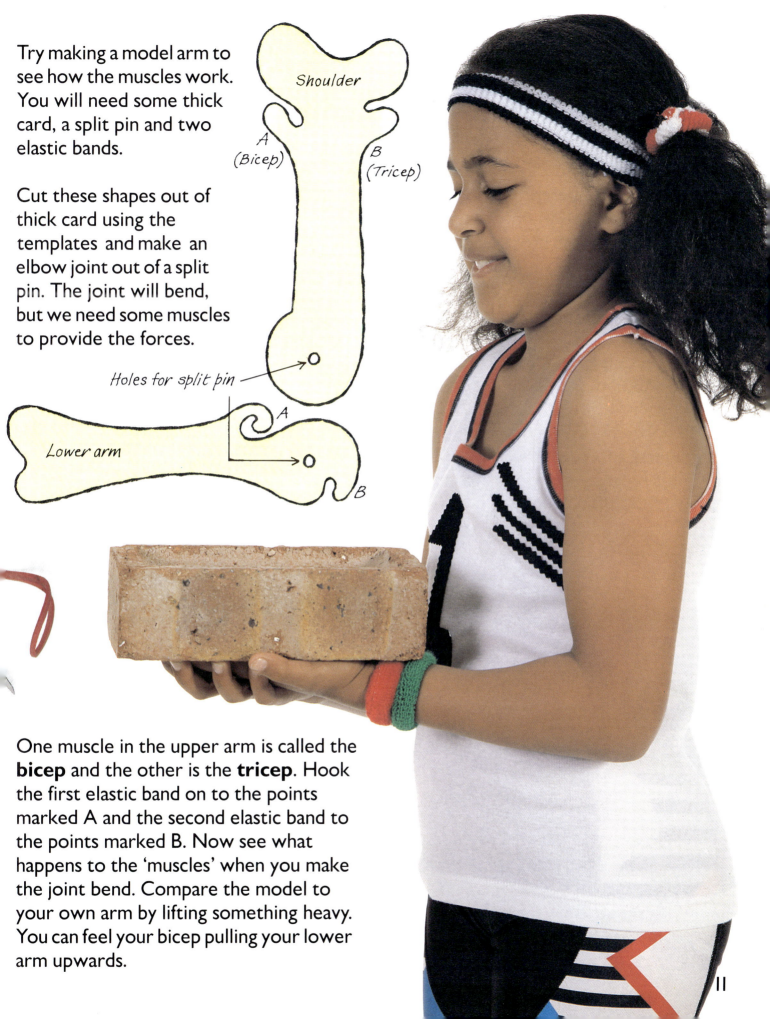

One muscle in the upper arm is called the **bicep** and the other is the **tricep**. Hook the first elastic band on to the points marked A and the second elastic band to the points marked B. Now see what happens to the 'muscles' when you make the joint bend. Compare the model to your own arm by lifting something heavy. You can feel your bicep pulling your lower arm upwards.

FORCES IN THE PLAYGROUND

Forces can be great fun. Visit a playground to see what you can do with different types of force. Remember always to be careful when you are playing on the equipment as you can be moving very fast and the ground is likely to be very hard.

▶ Try a swing. By moving your legs backwards and forwards, you can make the swing go up higher and higher. There is a force called **gravity** that pulls you downwards until you are at the bottom again.

▼ Next, have a ride on the roundabout. As it turns you can feel a force pulling on your body. This is a force that keeps you moving in a circle.

▶ Now try the slide. Let go and gravity does all the work for you, pulling you downwards. Look at the surface of the slide. To work best, it has to be very smooth so that you can slip down it easily. What do you think would happen if the slide had a rough surface?

Balance a tray against several building blocks or books to make a ramp. Choose a selection of heavy and light objects and try sliding them from the top of the tray. Do some things slide down more quickly than others? Do the objects slide faster if you wet the tray? Take away some of the blocks or books to change the slope of the tray. What difference does this make to how things will slide?

SLOWING DOWN

Whenever things touch there is always a special force that stops them from slipping. This force is called **friction**. If it was not for friction, the world would be a very strange place. Everything would keep sliding. Imagine what would happen if we tried to move. Our shoes would not grip the floor and we would fall over.

In some places friction is helpful and in others we try to get rid of it so that things move more easily. You can find lots of examples of friction on a bicycle.

Turn a bicycle upside-down and turn the pedals until the back **wheel** is spinning really fast. How long does it take for the wheel to slow down and stop? The **ball bearings** inside the centre of the wheel make a lot of noise because they rub together. Friction between the ball bearings slows the wheel down. If you put some grease on the ball bearings the wheel will turn more easily by making the friction less.

▼ Have a look at the chain. If you put **oil**, which is a slippery liquid, on it, the chain will move easily over the cogs to spin the wheels round.

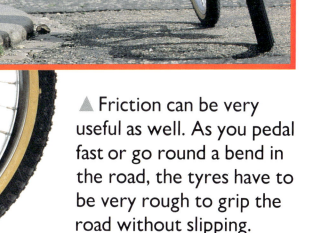

▲ Friction can be very useful as well. As you pedal fast or go round a bend in the road, the tyres have to be very rough to grip the road without slipping.

There is one place where friction is very important. If you want to stop quickly, your bicycle brakes have to provide a very large force. There is a lot of friction between the rubber brake blocks and the metal wheel rims.

There are many other examples of friction on a bicycle. See if you can find out where they are. You must look after your bike and keep it in good condition, as you never know when you are going to need friction.

MOVING FAST

There is also friction when things move in air or water. Friction with the air is called **drag**. Can you see how racing cars are specially shaped? A smooth, **streamlined** design cuts down the amount of friction and the cars move very fast.

▲ This boat has been designed to cut through the water very quickly. It too has a curved, streamlined hull that is very smooth so there is little friction. The water glides easily over the surface of the hull so that the boat can skim fast over the waves.

▶ Have you ever rubbed your hands together to keep warm on a cold day? As you move your hands, the friction makes heat. In the same way, when space rockets return to Earth, the friction with the air makes them get very hot on the outside. Space rockets are covered with special heatproof tiles to keep the astronauts cool.

BIG MACHINES

Maybe you could ask an adult to take you to visit a building site. You would see lots of huge machines there. Imagine how difficult it would be to build houses, schools, shops and offices without them.

These big machines use powerful forces. On these pages you can see a machine that mixes cement and another that scoops up earth rather like a giant shovel.

Did you know that paste is a type of cement? You can make your own paste to stick your paper models together.

Measure out one mug of flour and three mugs of water.

In a saucepan, mix a little of the water with the flour to make a smooth paste.

Add the rest of the water and ask an adult to heat the mixture until it boils – it must be stirred all the time! Turn the heat down and let the mixture simmer until the paste thickens.

GEARWHEELS ARE GREAT

Many machines use **gearwheels** to run properly. Big machines like cars and small machines like clocks both have them in their workings. Most gearwheels are made of metal so that they last longer. Oil keeps them cool as they turn and work.

▶ Look at this enlarged picture of the inside of a wind-up wristwatch. Lifesize, the gearwheels are very small but they make the hands of the watch travel around the watch face at the right speed. The ticking the watch makes is the noise of the gearwheels moving. Digital watches have different insides and do not use gearwheels. What watch do you have?

A gearwheel, or cog, has teeth around its edges that mesh, or lock, into those of another wheel. When one wheel moves round, it makes its neighbouring wheel turn as well.

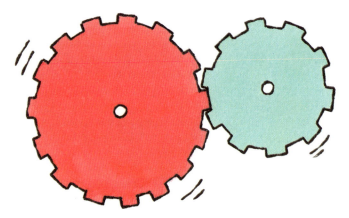

Gearwheels move power from one part of a machine to another. They can also be used to make parts turn faster or slower.

This windmill uses gearwheels to turn its sails. If you have a building kit with gearwheels, try building a model using one, two, three or more. Does it become harder or easier to turn the parts of your model with fewer or more gearwheels? Can you think of any machines around your home that use gearwheels?

ROLLERS AND PULLEYS

One way of moving things about is to drag them. This can be difficult because you create friction when you tug an object over the ground. Putting oil on a smooth floor would lessen the friction, but it would be very messy and people might fall over.

▼ You can make a thing easier to move by putting it on **rollers**, such as rolling pins or pencils. Can you see how this works? Instead of scraping along the ground, the box now rolls along, as there is not much friction.

▲ Pulleys are wheels with ropes around them. They are used on building sites to lift heavy loads.

◀ You can pull something with a really large amount of force by making a pulley. Here is a trick that makes you stronger than two friends. You need about six metres of rope, two broomsticks and two strong friends. Ask them to face each other holding a broomstick each. Now tie the end of the rope to one broomstick and thread the rope around both broomsticks five times. If you pull on the rope, you should be able to force your friends together. No matter how hard they pull apart, you will always be stronger.

▼ Obviously round rollers work very well, but did you know that rollers do not have to be circular to roll evenly? These shapes make just as good rollers.

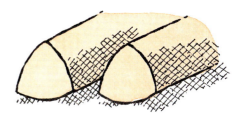

LEVERS

A **lever** can turn a small force into a big one. There are lots of examples of levers around the house.

▶ A spanner pushes a nut around with a very big force.

◀ It is very difficult to crack a nut with your hands, but a nutcracker gives you the force to do it.

▶ Tell your friends that you are strong enough to lift them with one hand. Can you think how to do it with a lever? Put a long, thick plank of wood on the ground with a brick a short distance from one end. If your friends stand on the short end just beyond the brick, it is easy to lift them by pushing on the other end of the plank. What would happen if they stood on the other end? Move the brick closer to the middle of the plank. Is it harder or easier to lift your friends?

FAST FOOD

Why do we need to eat? Food is very important. It does much more than just taste nice and stop us from feeling hungry. Food gives us energy to live, run and jump, just as cars and trains need fuel to move. If we do not eat enough food, we feel tired and grumpy.

There are different types of food. We need to eat some from each type to keep healthy. The types are called carbohydrates, proteins and fats.

Rice, bread and potatoes are all foods that give us **energy**. They are called carbohydrates. Before a long race, marathon runners have a pasta party. They eat platefuls of spaghetti to give them energy to run.

Athletes eat a lot of food containing proteins to make their bodies strong. Proteins are found in cheese, grains, meat and beans.

People also need to eat some fats from foods like milk, margarine, and ice cream.

If you want to stay healthy, try not to eat too many foods like cake, sweets, butter or chips. Your body does not need these to stay alive. Fish, fruit and vegetables are all good for you. Some people do not eat meat. They stay healthy by eating other food containing proteins. What did you eat today?

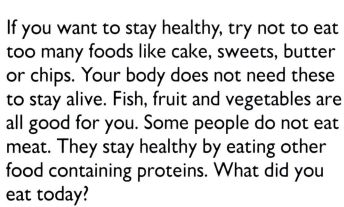

Children need to drink half a litre of milk every day to keep teeth and bones healthy.

GRAVITY

There is a force that pulls everything downwards, towards the Earth. It is called gravity. Imagine what it would be like without it. Walking would be impossible because your feet would not touch the floor. Things would not stay where you left them because they would be floating around the room like an astronaut.

Sometimes gravity can be a nuisance. When things fall, they can break when they hit the ground, like an egg hitting the kitchen floor.

Some things bounce. You can make a really bouncy ball in your own kitchen. You need some glue like the sort you use at school (called PVA or Poly Vinyl Alcohol) and some borax, which you can buy at a chemist.

▶ Put one teaspoon of borax in a teacup and dissolve it in two teaspoons of warm water. Then add one tablespoon of glue and mix it very quickly into the borax. Shape the glue in your hands and what happens? The runny glue becomes like a bouncy rubber ball.

▼ Add food colours to make your ball prettier. Try putting more or less borax in the mixture and see if it makes the ball even bouncier.
Be careful with your ball – it could stain the furniture.

GLOSSARY

Ball bearings are metal balls used to reduce friction.

Bicep is a muscle which raises the forearm.

Drag is friction in air.

Elastic things can stretch and then return to their original size. Elastic bands can be used to store power.

Energy is needed by all things to be active.

Force is a push or pull on an object.

Friction is a force that slows down a moving object.

Gearwheels (cogs) are toothed wheels.

Gravity is a force that pulls things towards the ground.

Joints are where bones meet.

Levers can lift heavy objects, like a see-saw.

Moving is not being still.

Muscles are parts of the body that pull on bones and help you to move.

Oil is a slippery liquid.

Pulley is a wheel with a rope around it, used for lifting heavy objects.

Rocket is a vehicle built to travel in space.

Rollers can be used to move a heavy object over a surface more easily. They turn smoothly and lessen the friction between the object and the surface.

Skeleton is the bones that give a body its shape.

Streamlined means shaped to travel quickly.

Tricep is the muscle that pulls the forearm down.

Wheels are circular rollers.

Windmill is a machine that works by wind power.

INDEX

aeroplane 5
arm 11

ball bearing 14
bicep 11
bicycle 14, 15
bicycle chain 14
bird 4
boat 16
bouncy ball 29
building site 18, 19

car 4
castle 22, 23
crane 19

drag 16

food 26, 27
force 6
friction 14, 15

gearwheel 20, 21
gravity 28, 29

indoor rocket 6

joint 10, 11

lever 24, 25

muscle 10, 11

nutcracker 24

oil 14

playground 12, 13
pulley 22, 23

racing car 16
roller 22
roundabout 13

skeleton 10
slide 12
space rocket 17
spanner 24
streamlining 16
swing 12

toy car 7
tricep 11
tyre 15

wheel 14
windmill 9, 21

For more information about TWO-CAN books, write to TWO-CAN Publishing, 346 Old Street, London, EC1V 9NQ.